D1540737

JU

MORNING GLORIES

MORNING GLORIES

by Sylvia A. Johnson

Photographs by Yuko Sato

A Lerner Natural Science Book

Lerner Publications Company ▪ Minneapolis

J
583.94
JOH

Sylvia A. Johnson, Series Editor

Translation of original text by Chaim Uri

The publisher wishes to thank Roberta Sladky, Department of Botany, University of Minnesota, for her assistance in the preparation of this book.

Additional photographs courtesy of: p. 18, Shabo Hani; p. 19, Masaharu Suzuki

The glossary on page 45 gives definitions and pronunciations of words shown in **bold type** in the text.

LIBRARY OF CONGRESS CATALOGING IN PUBLICATION DATA

Johnson, Sylvia A.
  Morning glories.

  (A Lerner natural science book)
  Adaptation of: Asagao/photographs by Yuko Sato; text by Shuhei Nakayama.
  Includes index.
  Summary: Examines the lives of morning glories and the stages of development leading to the production of their delicate flowers.
  1. Morning glories—Juvenile literature. 2. Morning glories—Development—Juvenile literature. 3. Plants—Development—Juvenile literature. [1. Morning glories. 2. Plants—Development] I. Satō, Yūko, 1928-   ill. II. Nakayama, Shūhei. Asagao. III. Title. IV. Series.
  QK495.C78J64 1985   583'.79   85-12970
  ISBN 0-8225-1462-1 (lib. bdg.)

This edition first published 1985 by Lerner Publications Company.
Text copyright © 1985 by Lerner Publications Company.
Photographs copyright © 1972 by Yuko Sato.
Text adapted from MORNING GLORIES: FROM SEEDS TO SEEDS copyright © 1972 by Shuhei Nakayama.
English language rights arranged by Japan Foreign-Rights Centre for Akane Shobo Publishers, Tokyo, Japan.

All rights to this edition reserved by Lerner Publications Company.
International copyright secured. Manufactured in the United States of America.

International Standard Book Number: 0-8225-1462-1
Library of Congress Catalog Number: 85-12970

1 2 3 4 5 6 7 8 9 10 95 94 93 92 91 90 89 88 87 86 85

The delicate blossoms are shaped like trumpets and colored in pinks and lavenders and blues. They grow on vines that twine around fence posts and porch rails, covering the stiff wood with a graceful cascade of flowers and bright green leaves. The plants are morning glories, a familiar sight in gardens and along country roads in many parts of the world.

In this book, we will take a close look at the secret lives of morning glories and at the stages of development that lead to the production of the lovely flowers for which the plants are famous.

Developing roots break through the seed coats of morning-glory seeds planted in the earth.

SEEDS

The life story of a morning-glory plant begins with something very small and insignificant—a single hard, dry seed. Planted in soil and supplied with warmth and moisture, this tiny seed can develop into a complete new plant.

As it absorbs water from the soil, the morning-glory seed begins to swell. Soon pressure from the inside causes a tiny opening to widen in the **seed coat**, the tough outer covering of the seed. Out of this opening emerges a thin white thread. It is a developing root, called a **radicle**.

The radicle makes its appearance about six days after the seed was planted. It is a sign that the seed has **germinated** and that the new morning-glory plant has started to grow.

As the tiny root extends deeper into the soil, another section of the growing plant begins to push above the surface. This region, called the **hypocotyl**, forms the connection between the root and the seed. It will eventually develop into the plant's stem.

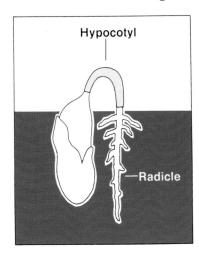

Seven days after planting, the hypocotyl has arched upward until it has broken through the surface of the soil. The new plant has begun to reach out toward the sunlight and air that will be vital to its continued growth.

In the first stage of the plant's development, the root and the hypocotyl begin to lengthen and grow. As the root extends down into the soil, the hypocotyl arches up above the surface (above). Exposed to sunlight, this part of the developing plant takes on a reddish color (opposite). Hidden within the darkness of the soil, the white root pushes steadily downward in search of life-giving moisture.

ROOTS

It is not surprising that the root is the first part of the morning glory to develop fully. Roots are very important to the life of any plant. They provide an anchor that supports the plant and allows it to grow tall. They also take in water and minerals that are essential to healthy growth.

Like all plant roots, the root of a morning-glory plant has special features that enable it to do its job efficiently. The growing tip of the root is covered by a **root cap**, a loose collection of cells that fits over the end of the root like a cap or thimble. As the root pushes through the soil, the root cap protects its delicate tip from damage.

Root hairs are another special feature of plant roots. These tiny, hair-like projections cover the lower part of the root above the root cap. Root hairs begin to grow early in the root's development. They play a vital role in helping to satisfy the young plant's need for water. The millions of hairs take in water from the soil, each one acting as a tiny tube in carrying the precious liquid to the root. The root in turn conducts the water to the other parts of the plant.

Nine days after the morning-glory seed was put into the soil, these other parts of the plant are growing rapidly. By now, the first green leaves are flourishing above the surface of the earth.

The first leaves of two developing plants emerge from the soil.

LEAVES

The morning glory's first leaves are pulled from the soil by the movement of the hypocotyl. As the plant grows, the hypocotyl begins to straighten up from its earlier arched position. This straightening movement pulls two thick green leaves out of the seed coat, where they have been stored. Supported by the developing stem, the leaves emerge into the light of day.

12

The seed coat, adorned with a drop of water, is still attached to these new leaves. As the leaves expand, the empty seed coat will drop off.

13

Left: The cotyledons of a morning-glory plant are thick leaves with deep notches in them. *Opposite:* Between the two cotyledons of this morning glory can be seen a small green knob that will soon develop into the plants's first true leaves.

The first leaves of the morning glory play a special role in the plant's development. Known as **seed leaves** or **cotyledons**, they have a different function from the "true" leaves that will appear later.

Cotyledons are storage places for food energy. They contain protein, starch, and other substances that nourish the growing plant. All the early growth of the morning glory, beginning with the germination of the seed, was made possible by nutrients contained in the cotyledons. These special "seed" leaves will continue to nourish the young plant until the growth of true leaves, which will take over the job of supplying food.

Like many other flowering plants, the morning glory has two cotyledons. Botanists, scientists who study plants, refer to it as a **dicot** because of this characteristic. Other dicots include such familiar garden plants as roses, peonies, and peas, as well as many common trees and shrubs. **Monocots**, plants with only one cotyledon, are not as numerous as their dicot relatives. In this smaller group are lilies, orchids, and grasses like wheat and rice.

Sunsbury Public Library
Children's Room

As the nutrients stored in the cotyledons are used up, the morning glory's true leaves begin to develop. The first true leaves grow from between the cotyledons, as you can see in the photograph on the preceding page. They emerge from the **terminal bud**, which is located at the top of the developing plant's stem.

The morning glory shown below has two true leaves (center) in addition to its cotelydons. The true leaves are shaped differently than the seed leaves, and they have a very different function in the life of the plant.

As the plant continues to develop, more and more true leaves emerge. They grow from the stem at points called **nodes**. In morning glories, only one leaf is produced by each node. (This can be seen clearly in the photograph on the opposite page.)

Scientists call this arrangement of leaves **alternate**. Other flowering plants such as the rose have an **opposite** arrangement, with two leaves growing from each node at opposite sides of the stem.

Both alternate and opposite leaves grow in a spiral pattern around the plant stem so that new leaves do not emerge directly above older ones. This allows all the leaves to receive as much sunlight as possible.

The enlarged photograph on the right shows the pores or stomata in a morning-glory leaf (left). Each pore is surrounded by two long guard cells.

Sunlight is the energy source that provides fuel for the young plant's food-producing system. Like all green plants, a morning-glory plant makes food through the process of **photosynthesis**. This word literally means "putting together with light," and that is exactly what the leaves of a plant do. They produce food by using the energy of the sun to combine raw materials drawn from the soil and the air.

The basic ingredients that a plant needs for photosynthesis are carbon dioxide, water, and, of course, sunlight. Carbon dioxide is a gas given off by living things during the process of respiration. It is taken into a plant's leaves through tiny openings or pores called **stomata**. The other essential ingredient, water, is drawn up from the soil through the roots.

The combining of water and carbon dioxide to form food requires

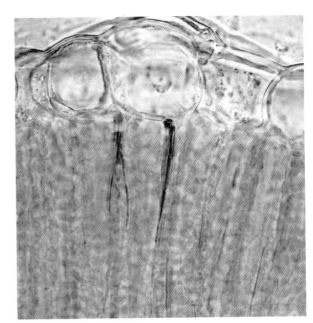

In this cross-section photograph of a plant leaf, you can see the green pigment chlorophyll contained in the long, thin palisade cells below the leaf's surface. Above them are the colorless cells of the upper epidermis.

a complex chemical process that takes place in the cells of a plant's leaves. Within these cells are tiny bodies called **chloroplasts**, containing the green pigment **chlorophyll**. Chlorophyll is the material that gives plants their green color, but it also plays a vital role in photosynthesis.

By absorbing sunlight, chlorophyll produces the energy that breaks down and then combines the molecules of water and carbon dioxide. The results of this synthesis are two new substances— oxygen and a form of sugar known as **glucose**.

Glucose is the basic food used by a plant in growing, reproducing, and carrying on all of its life processes. The plant also uses some oxygen, but most of this gas is released through the stomata into the atmosphere. Here it supplies the essential element for the respiration of all forms of animal life, including human beings.

STEMS

As the leaves of the morning-glory plant begin to produce large amounts of food through photosynthesis, the new plant grows quickly. Its stem becomes long and thin, reaching up toward the sun.

Morning glories are vining plants, and their stems need support in order to remain upright. If a plant is near a pole or post, it will wind its stem around it, clinging to the wood stubbornly. Like most vining plants, the morning glory twists around the pole in a counter-clockwise direction, always turning to the left. You can see that characteristic in the photographs on these two pages.

The plant in the photograph on the right has been marked with ink to demonstrate another interesting feature of the morning-glory's growth. The ink marks were first put on the stem at equal distances from each other, but as the plant grew, the marks on the upper portion of the stem became further apart than those on the lower section.

This happens because the plant's upward growth is taking place only in the top part of the stem. New cells are constantly being added at the **apical meristem**, the actively growing area at the stem's tip. Once formed, these new cells enlarge and cause the stem to lengthen in the area immediately below the tip. Further down, no new growth takes place, and the space between the ink marks does not increase.

Left: An axillary bud growing in a leaf axil. *Opposite:* The bud gradually develops into a branch.

As new cells are added at the morning glory's apical meristem, new nodes and leaves are continually developing on the upper portion of the stem. The stem also increases slightly in width through the production of new cells along its outside surfaces. There is another way in which the plant grows, and that is by adding branches.

A branch usually grows from an **axillary bud**. This tiny structure develops in a leaf **axil**, the angle formed at the spot where the leaf stalk or **petiole** joins the stem. (The photograph above shows an axil with an axillary bud.) As the bud grows, it turns into a miniature stem, with all the features of the plant's main stem. In fact, a branch is nothing more than a secondary stem, capable, like the main stem, of producing leaves, flowers, and even other stems.

Left and opposite: Flower buds appear on a morning-glory plant.

FLOWERS

It is now more than two months since the morning-glory seed was put into the ground. The plant has been growing vigorously, producing new leaves and branches at a rapid rate. By mid-summer, the morning glory has completed this **vegetative phase** of growth and is ready to enter a new stage in its development.

The beginning of this new stage is marked by the appearance of a different kind of bud at the ends of branches, in the leaf axils, and around the nodes. These buds are larger than the other plant buds, and they do not develop into new leaves or branches. Instead they become flowers, the beautiful pink and lavender blossoms of the morning-glory plant.

Flower buds first appear on the lower part of the stem, which is the oldest section of the plant. As the warm summer days pass, more and more of the delicate trumpets begin to open on the morning-glory vine.

Above and opposite: The gradual opening of a morning-glory flower

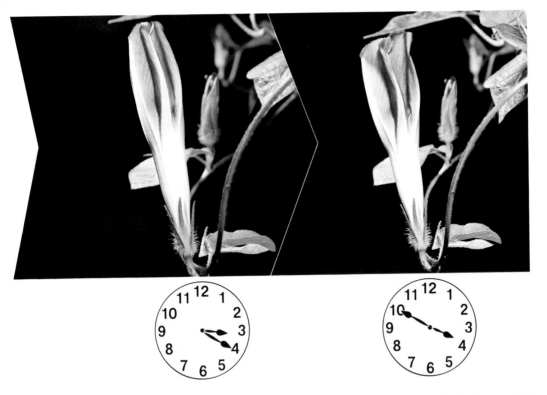

Morning glories were given their name because their beautiful flowers are definitely creatures of the morning. Each individual blossom usually opens very early in the day, and by the time that the afternoon sun is at its hottest, it has already wilted and died.

The photographs on these two pages and on the following page show the gradual opening of a morning-glory flower. By three A.M. on a balmy summer night, when the sky is still black, the tightly twisted petals have already begun to unfurl (left). As the minutes pass, the blossom slowly unfolds until the vivid pink of its petals can be seen (above). At four o'clock, before the light of the sun has begun to redden the sky, the morning glory is completely open, its petals spread in radiant color (next page).

The corolla of a morning-glory flower is supported by five or six green sepals.

When the blossoms of a morning glory begin to open in the cool of a summer morning, the plant has entered the **reproductive phase** of its life. The flowers that humans find so graceful and appealing play a very practical role in the morning glory's development. They make it possible for the plant to produce offspring and to pass on its genes to a new generation of morning glories.

Like all flowering plants, a morning glory reproduces sexually. New morning glories are created by the union of male and female sex cells. Just like animals, flowering plants have special reproductive organs that produce sex cells. These organs are contained in a plant's flowers.

A morning glory's reproductive organs are hidden within the narrow tube at the base of the flower. This tube is formed by the fusing of the flower's five petals. At the top, the tube flares out, and you can see the divisions that mark the five separate petals. The tube of petals is known as the flower's **corolla**, and it is supported by the **calyx**, made up of leaf-like green **sepals**.

29

Opposite: This photograph shows the reproductive parts of a morning-glory flower.

In order to get a good look at the morning glory's reproductive parts, it is necessary to cut away the top section of the flower's corolla. That is what has been done in the photograph on the opposite page. The white, stalk-like objects are the sex organs of the flower.

Many flowering plants, including the morning glory, have both male and female organs on one flower. The **pistil**, the female organ, rises up in the center of the flower. Around it are clustered a number of **stamens**, the male organs of the flower.

At the base of the pistil is a hollow chamber, or **ovary**, which contains tiny structures known as **ovules**. Within each ovule is an **egg**, the female sex cell. **Sperm**, or male sex cells, develop within microscopic grains of pollen manufactured by the **anthers** at the tips of the stamens. It is the union of these male and female cells that begins the development of a new generation of plants.

In many kinds of morning-glory plants, the sex cells produced by a single flower do not normally unite. The stamens and pistil often develop at different times so that when pollen is being manufactured, the **stigma** at the tip of the pistil is not ready to receive it. In order to begin the process of reproduction, the flower must receive pollen from flowers of another morning-glory plant in a different stage of development. To accomplish this, it needs help from the insect world.

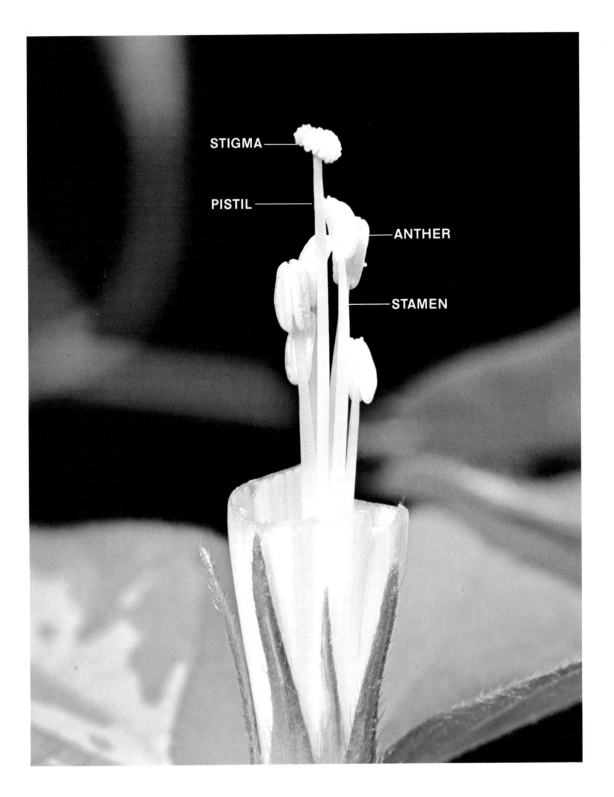

Searching for nectar, a swallowtail butterfly pollinates a morning-glory flower.

Insects like this swallowtail butterfly are the most important **pollinators** of morning-glory plants. Probing with their long mouthparts deep in a flower's corolla, butterflies search for the sweet nectar that the morning glory produces. In the process, they pick up grains of golden pollen on their bodies and wings. As the insects enter other morning glories seeking nectar, the pollen rubs off on stigmas that are ready to receive it. When this happens, the flowers have been **pollinated**.

The next step in the process of reproduction is **fertilization**, the actual union of male sperm and female eggs. This takes place when pollen grains on the stigma split open and form tiny tubes. These hollow **pollen tubes** grow downward through the **style**, the stalk joining the stigma to the ovary. Sperm cells pass down the tubes and enter the ovules in the ovary. Here they unite with, or fertilize, the egg cells. This union is the beginning of another generation of morning-glory plants.

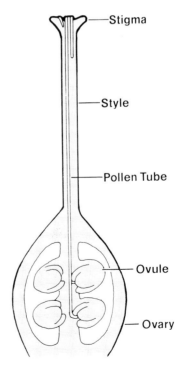

Stigma

Style

Pollen Tube

Ovule

Ovary

Opposite: While some flowers on this morning-glory plant have wilted, others have not yet opened. The plant will continue to produce blossoms throughout the warm months of summer.

Since each morning-glory flower blooms for only one day, some blossoms do not receive a visit from pollinating insects and therefore miss the opportunity for fertilization. But each day, new flowers on the plant open their bright petals and spread their delicate fragrance on the warm air. The morning-glory vine will continue to produce blooms throughout the summer, and many of the flowers will attract insect pollinators before their day in the sun is over.

After each flower dies, its petals wilt and fall to the ground, but the green sepals and the flower ovary remain on the stem. At this point, the ovaries of the flowers that have been fertilized undergo a change. They enlarge, and their walls become thicker and harder. This change marks the beginning of a new stage in the plant's development. The ovaries and some of the flower parts around them have become the **fruits** of the morning glory.

Unlike the large, juicy fruits of apple trees or tomato plants, the fruit or **capsule** of the morning glory is small and dry. Despite this difference, it plays exactly the same role in the life of the plant: it encloses and protects the precious seeds that are developing inside.

The fruits of a morning-glory plant

SEEDS

Like the seeds of all flowering plants, morning-glory seeds develop from the ovules. Through the process of cell divison, the fertilized eggs in the ovules gradually grow into **embryos**, tiny plants-to-be. Each embryo is made up of a shoot with the developing root, or radicle, at one end and two cotyledons at the other end.

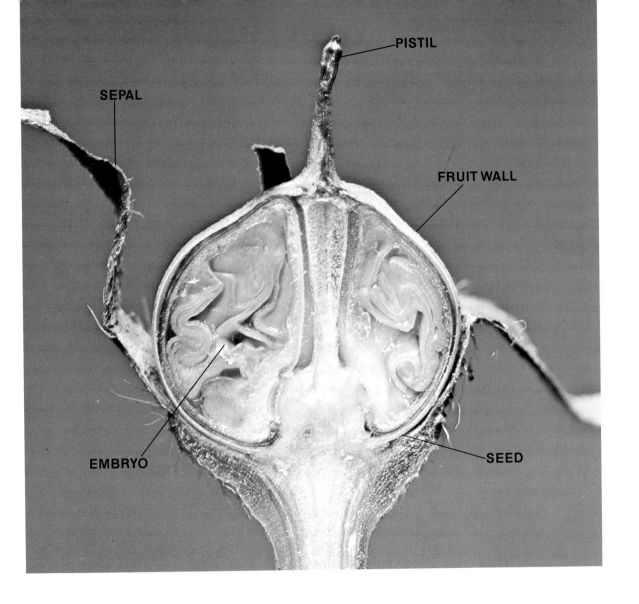

PISTIL

SEPAL

FRUIT WALL

EMBRYO

SEED

As you can see in the photograph above, these miniature parts of the embryo plant are folded tightly inside the seed, which is in turn enclosed by the morning-glory fruit. (In this photograph, the fruit has been cut in half lengthwise, revealing the contents of two developing seeds.)

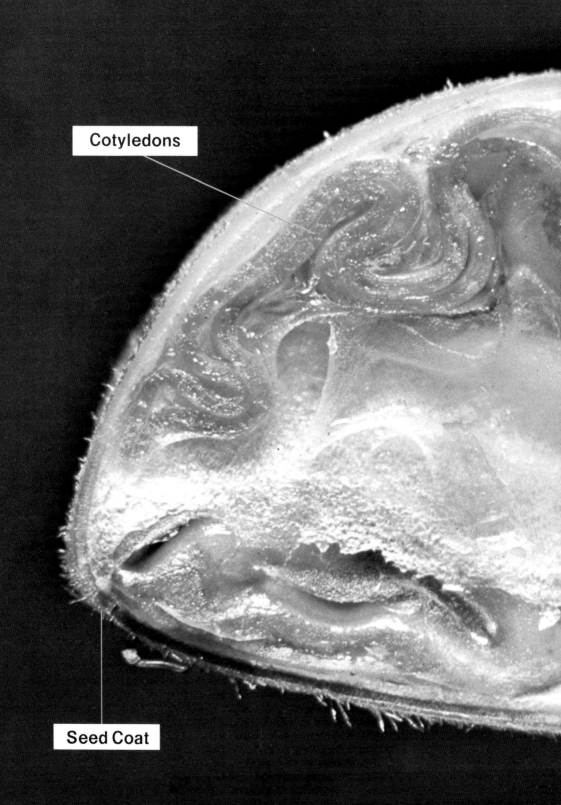

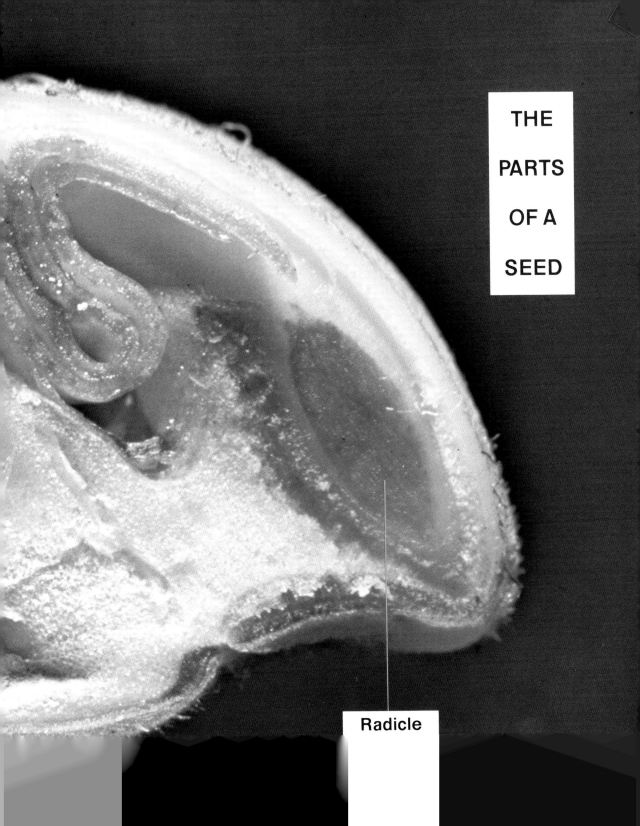

THE

PARTS

OF A

SEED

Radicle

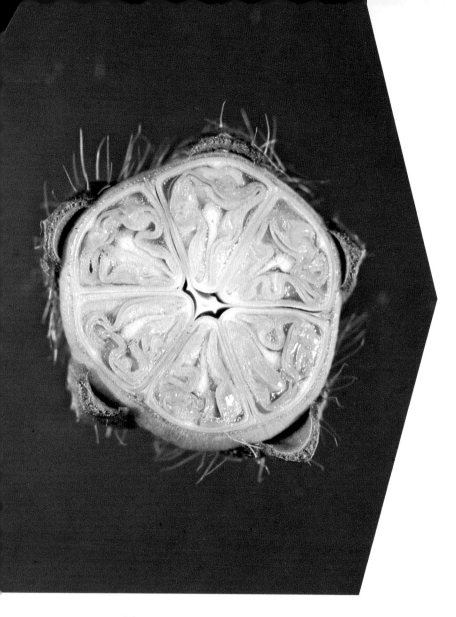

This morning-glory fruit was cut crosswise and photographed from above to show the six seeds packed tightly inside. In this early stage of the fruit's development, the fruit wall and the seeds are plump and moist. The embryo plants within the seeds are bright green.

You will notice that this fruit has only five seeds instead of six. One ovule did not develop into a seed, probably because it was not fertilized or because it had some serious flaw that prevented its growth.

This is a morning-glory fruit in a later stage of growth. Its outer wall is dry and hard. The seeds inside have lost their green color and have developed hard, dark seed coats. They are preparing for a period of inactivity, or **dormancy**, before they return to active life.

The seeds of a morning-
glory plant

By the end of the summer, the morning-glory vine has become dry and brittle. All the green leaves have withered, and the brilliant flowers are only a memory, gone like the warm winds of July. Some of the fruits still cling to the plant stem, while others have fallen and lie scattered on the ground. As autumn advances, the dry and papery fruit capsules split open, releasing the black seeds.

A few of the morning-glory seeds remain on the ground near the parent plant, while others are washed away by heavy autumn rains. Some seeds are picked up by ants and buried underground as part of their winter food supply. Seeds from garden plants may be collected by humans and saved for planting in the spring.

Of the thousands of seeds produced by one plant, at least a few will survive the rains of autumn and the cold of winter, the life within them protected by the tough seed coat. In the returning warmth of spring, they will germinate and produce a new generation of bright-flowered morning-glory plants.

The colorful blossoms of some cultivated morning glories

THE MORNING-GLORY FAMILY

Morning glories belong to the scientific family Convolvulaceae, a group made up of an interesting variety of plants. In addition to the many species of cultivated morning glories, the family includes some wild relatives with very unusual habits.

Bindweed is a kind of wild morning glory belonging to the genus *Convovulus.* This plant gets its common name because of its habit of binding itself tightly to the support it grows on. Various species of bindweeds can be found in fields and hedges in many parts of the world.

Dodder, another member of the family Convolvulaceae, also gets a tight grip on supporting vegetation but with much more damaging results than the harmless bindweed. This relative of the morning glory is a parasite, a plant that gets its nourishment from other plants. A dodder has no leaves, and it contains no chlorophyll. Its yellow or white stems twist around supporting plants, piercing them with special branches that absorb water and nutrients. In Europe, several different species of dodders (all members of the genus *Cuscuta)* frequently cause serious crop damage.

There is another close relative of the morning glory that produces food instead of destroying it. It is the sweet potato, which is a member of the same genus, *Ipomoea*, that includes cultivated morning glories. The vining sweet potato plant has a thick yellowish root that is rich in starch and vitamins. This nourishing root was first used as a food by the Indians of South America. The cultivated white potato, which also originated in this part of the world, belongs to a completely different plant family.

GLOSSARY

alternate—a pattern of plant growth in which only one leaf grows from each stem node

anthers—the enlarged tips of stamens, where pollen is produced

apical meristem (AY-pih-kuhl MER-ih-stem)—the actively growing area at the tip of a plant stem, branch, or leaf

axil (AK-sil)—the angle formed between a leaf and the stem on which it grows

axillary (AK-seh-ler-ee) bud—a bud that grows in a leaf axil

calyx (KAY-liks)—the part of the flower made up of sepals

capsule—a dry fruit that splits open to release the plant seeds

chlorophyll (KLOR-uh-fil)—a green pigment that absorbs sunlight, producing the energy that makes photosynthesis possible

chloroplasts (KLOR-uh-plasts—tiny bodies in plant cells that contain chlorophyll

corolla (kuh-ROHL-eh)—the part of the flower formed by the petals

cotyledons (kaht-'l-EED-uns)—the leaves of an embryo plant, which serve as storage places for food energy; seed leaves

dicots (DI-kots)—plants with two cotyledons

dormancy (DOR-muhn-see)—a period of inactivity before germination

embryos (EM-bree-ohs)—immature plants that develop within seeds

fertilization—the union of male sperm cells and female egg cells

fruits—the parts of a plant that enclose and protect the seeds

germinate (JER-mih-nate)—to begin growing

glucose (GLU-kose) — a form of sugar produced by plants during photosynthesis

hypocotyl (HI-puh-kot'l) — the part of a plant embryo that develops into the stem

monocots (MON-uh-kots) — plants with one cotyledon

nodes (NODES) — the points on a stem where leaves are attached

opposite — a pattern of plant growth in which a pair of leaves grows from each stem node

ovary — the hollow chamber at the base of the pistil where seeds are formed

ovules (AHV-yuls) — tiny structures in a flower ovary that can develop into seeds

petiole (PET-ee-ohl) — the thin stalk of a leaf

photosynthesis (fot-uh-SIN-thih-sis) — the process by which green plants use the energy of the sun to make food

pistil — the female reproductive organ of a flower

pollen tubes — tiny tubes that carry sperm cells from the stigma into the ovary

pollinators — animals that carry pollen from one flower to another

radicle (RAD-ih-kuhl) — the part of a plant embryo that develops into the root

reproductive phase — the stage in a plant's development during which flowers and seeds are produced

root cap — a loose collection of cells that fits over the end of a root and protects it from damage

root hairs — tiny hair-like structures on the root that take in water from the soil

seed coat—the tough outer covering of a seed

seed leaves—the leaves of an embryo plant, serving as storage places for food energy; cotyledons

sepals (SEE-pahls)—the leaf-like structures that support a flower's corolla

stamens (STAY-muhns)—the male reproductive organs of a flower

stigma—the sticky tip of the pistil

stomata (STO-muh-tuh)—the tiny pores or openings in a plant leaf. The singular form of the word is **stoma.**

style—the stalk connecting the stigma to the ovary

terminal bud—the bud at the tip of a plant stem

vegetative phase—the stage in a plant's development during which leaves are produced

INDEX

alternate leaves, 17
anthers, 30
apical meristem, 21, 22
axil, 22, 24
axillary bud, 22

bindweed, 44
branches, 22
bud, 22, 24

calyx, 29
capsule, 35, 42
carbon dioxide, 18-19
chlorophyll, 19
chloroplasts, 19
Convolvulaceae, 44
corolla, 29
cotyledons, 14, 16, 36

dicot, 15
dodder, 44
dormancy, 41

egg, 30, 33, 36
embryos, 36, 40

fertilization, 33, 35
flowers, 5, 42; development of, 24, 27; role of, 29, 30, 33, 35
fruit, 35, 37, 40, 41, 42

germination, 7, 14
glucose, 19

hypocotyl, 7, 8

insects, 33

leaves, 10, 42; arrangement of, 16, development of, 12, 16; role of, 14, 19

monocot, 14

nodes, 16, 22

opposite leaves, 17
ovary, 30, 33, 35
ovules, 30, 36
oxygen, 19

petiole, 22
photosynthesis, 18-19, 20
pistil, 30, 33
pollen, 30, 33
pollen tubes, 33
pollinators, 33

radicle, 7, 36
reproductive organs of flower, 29, 30
reproductive phase, 29
root, 7, 8, 10, 18, 36
root cap, 10
root hairs, 10

seed coat, 7, 12
seed leaves, 14
seeds, 35, 37, 40, 41, 42; development of, 35, 36; germination of, 7
sepals, 29, 35
sex cells, 29, 30
sperm, 30, 33
stamens, 30
stems, 7, 20; vining of, 20
stigma, 30, 33
stomata, 18, 19
style, 33
sunlight, 17, 18-19
sweet potato, 44

terminal bud, 16
true leaves, 16

vegetative phase, 24